To Pe

WARTS AN' ALL

An entertainment by Tom Power and Tom O'Brien

First printing

Published by tomtom-theatre

A Bar somewhere in rural Ireland

JOHN, an aged man, with a younger friend, MICK, in the bar, waiting for friend JACK, from England. MAGGIE is behind the bar.
All scenes take place in the bar

JOHN: Two pints please Maggie; I must say you're looking good tonight.

MAGGIE: Plamás will get you nowhere.

JOHN: You never know your luck in a strange town, if I was a day younger I'd ask you out.

MAGGIE: Maybe if you add a few years to that day I might think about it. You're in a good mood tonight, and this town isn't strange, the only thing strange 'round here is you and your books and poetry, I see you have a few of them with you.

JOHN: Yes Maggie, I'm in good mood, it's been a good day and hopefully a better night. I'm meeting a friend, Jack and his wife here tonight, well an internet friend, although we were in England at the same time years ago, I never met him or his wife, and the good news is, he's an author, playwright, and a poet as well, and good at them all.
We became friends through email, and exchanging our books and poems.
And would you believe, I was in Waterford today, and as I was walking up through the apple market, I heard someone call my name, I turned around, and there she was Tess, another friend I knew in England, and who I haven't seen for many years. I'm meeting her for a chat in the Tower Hotel tomorrow night. So tonight, Mick will sing a few songs, I will read a few poems and a page or two from my books and Jack will do the same, and a good time will be had by all, and maybe a dance or two.

MAGGIE: Here's your two pints, and don't save the last dance for me.

JOHN: Ah now Maggie, it's got to be rock 'n roll music if you want to dance with me, you can keep your ould line dancing, that's only for the older generation.

MAGGIE: Older generation? And you're not?

JOHN: Only on the outside Maggie...only on the outside. Come on Mick. Let's take these two pints to a quiet table, and you can tune up that guitar.

John and Mick at the table, Mick tuning his guitar, John taking a slug from his pint

JOHN: Ah. That's good I needed that.

MICK: How is your poetry C/D going?

JOHN: It's doing alright, it got a great review in the Munster Express from Liam Murphy, and the Americans love it, a shower of begrudgers around here, "I knew him when he had no arse in his trousers, and he thinning turnips at twelve, and now he's writing poetry, 'tis far from poetry he was reared."

MICK: The girl you met in town...her and you were ye? I mean...

JOHN: Ah Mick, spit it out, yes we were an item for a while... a beautiful girl, Tess.
I met her on the Easter Monday bank holiday, at the travelling fair on the edge of Hampstead Heath; there were always a fair there over the Easter bank holiday, merry-go -rounds, hurdy-gurdys, coconut stalls, swings, chair-o-planes, and of course the bumpers, all the fun of the fair as they say, you could say she bumped into me. I was showing my skills on the bumpers, when bang! From behind and there she was smiling at me.

MICK: Hang on; wait till I get a refill.

Mick goes to the bar.

MICK: Pull another two pints Maggie.

MAGGIE: John's in a good mood tonight, I'd never tell him, but his book is good, and I enjoy his poetry, I suppose he and his friend will read a few poems tonight.

MICK: I'm sure they will Maggie, and I'll sing a few songs. At his age, if you like his books and poetry, you should tell him, you may not get the chance again.

Mick brings the two pints to the table

MICK: Now oil your vocals cords with that, and tell me more about this fair.

JOHN: Ah yes, the famous Hampstead Easter fair, well as I was saying, she hit me a right clatter, and when I looked around there she was smiling at me, well needless to say I chased her down, and then we gave each other a right bashing around that circuit. I bought her candy floss, and won her a gold fish at the coco nut stall. That's how we met; we were together for about two months, nothing serious, just on and off, some weekends I'd see her, and other weekends she was...well, I don't know, somewhere else.

MICK: Or with someone else, what happened, did you break it off?

JOHN: No...No, I don't know what happened, we were dancing in the Galtymore on Saturday night, I told her I had to go to Birmingham on a job for a week, we arranged to meet in The Rifle Volunteer in Kilburn high road the following Saturday night, she never turned up. And I haven't seen her since. I enquired around; it was rumoured she had gone back to Ireland for a funeral, or something, maybe she stayed there. Anyway I moved back to Birmingham with the job, and stayed there for two years and then came back here.

MICK: Maybe she'll explain all tomorrow night.

JOHN: Maybe, Mick, maybe, anyway some good came out of it, that poem I wrote that you put a tune to; I wrote it a few weeks afterwards.

MICK: You mean, "Permanent Tear".

JOHN: That's the one.

MICK: Will I sing it now?

JOHN: Not yet Mick, wait till Jack gets here.

A man enters the pub, he looks around and John sees him

JOHN: Well, speak of the devil, I think that's him, Jack? Over here.

Jack walks to the table reaches out to shake hands with John

JACK: John? Yes it is you, I recognise you from your face book photo, great to meet you, and I've been looking forward to it.

JOHN: Me too, you're on your own?

JACK: Yes. Theresa, my wife is meeting Mary, a friend of hers, she dropped me off, and she'll call in later.

JOHN: This is my friend Mick, a musician and songwriter, he put a tune to a few of my poems.

MICK: Great to meet you, John has been telling me all about you it's not every day we have two writers in this neck of the woods.

JACK: Just dabblers Mick, dabblers, that's all.

5

MICK: Oh ye're more than dabblers, I've read your book "Cricklewood Cowboys", and I went to see your play "Johnjo", and I've read some of your poems, I've read John's two books, "The Mysterious John Grey", and "Dust Covered Memories" and I have his C/D "The Spoken Word".

JOHN: Let me get you a drink, what are you having?

JACK: A pint of Guinness.

John goes to the counter.

JOHN: Three pints of Guinness please Maggie.

MAGGIE: So that's your friend Jack, writer, playwright and poet.

JOHN: And he's good at it too.

MAGGIE: I'll take these to the table for you.

JOHN: Thanks Maggie.

John returns to the table.

JACK: I suppose we've done alright for turnip thinners John, especially outside of Ireland. How much a drill did they pay you?

JOHN: Hah! Pay? Farmers would pay ya nothing, boy! Only barely enough for a ticket on the cattle boat. Maybe it's because we are turnip thinners we haven't done well here, if we had a higher education we might be more successful here.

JACK: Nothing new in that John, it's in the bible, Luke...And I quote "Truly I say to you, no prophet is accepted in his homeland."

JOHN: I'll have to take your word for that, Jack!

MICK: I think here we are more inclined to judge people by their background, not on their work.

Maggie, coming towards the table, overhears

MAGGIE: I'd say prophets are scarce on the ground around here.

JOHN: Ah now Maggie, I'm sure many prophets down through the years have rested their elbow on that counter.

MAGGIE: They have exercised their elbow no doubt, the only thing you hear them prophesying around here is the latest price they might get from the Mart, the milk price from Glanbia, or who's going to win a hurling match, or what horse is going to win at Leopardstown.

JOHN: Speaking of Leopardstown... I was in a pub with a friend not far from here, we were discussing poetry and of course Yeats was mentioned. The barman overheard us and said, he had some win yesterday, did ye have him backed? I said, no, I didn't think he was in a fit state to run. He answered, oh he ran alright, and ran well, flew past the post. I got off the stool and said, "I will arise and go now." My friend said, to Innishfree? I answered, no, outside to bang my head of the wall a few times.

JACK: No wonder your brain is rattled, but bar rooms such as this, has provided many writers with inspiration down through the years. Behan, Dylan Thomas, Hemingway, Fitzgerald. Myles Na Gopaleen, and, of course, Paddy Kavanagh...

> You do not come down that road anymore
> Past the ash trees where the gap in the hedge revealed
> Your blue dress trimming to the bottom of Callan's field
> And the free-wheel of your bicycle likes the whirr
> Of the breeze in the black sallies. If you could see
> The clay of time falling away from my feet
> When you appeared this side of Callan's gate,
> You'd come.

Ah yes, Paddy wrote some of his greatest poetry while under the influence of Arthur Guinness.

MICK: And songwriters as well. Many a great lyric was found at the bottom of an empty whiskey bottle. Could a non drinker have written? "Sunday Morning Coming Down" could a snowball survive in hell? Christopherson was reliving his experience in that song.

JACK: And speaking of that great man Mick, would you sing that song for us?

Mick picks up and tunes his guitar, then sings

> On a Sunday morning sidewalks, wishin' lord, that I was stoned,
> 'Cause there's something in a Sunday, makes a body feel alone,
> And there's nothin' short of dyin', half as lonesome as the sound,
> On the sleepin' city sidewalks, Sunday mornin' comin' down...

JACK: Great Mick, that brings me back... Kilburn High Road, Camden Town, Shepherds Bush, and many the Irishman, smoking and coughing his way to the nearest pub for a cure, and company on Sunday morning

JOHN: Anyone who was ever drunk on a Saturday night can relate to that song. My friends and I used to meet in the Pembroke Arms in Chalk Farm on Sunday morning, pints of Guinness, and cheddar cheese and crackers on the counter, that was our breakfast, Kenny Rodgers and Ruby on the jukebox. You're right about the company Jack, bedsits, or dosshouses can be lonely places, the pub provided company. Was that what Pierce and Connelly and their comrades fought for? So that Ireland's sons and daughters could get pissed in some lonely city on a Saturday night, Ireland answer to unemployment...emigration, to England, Australia, America, or any part of the world where work was to be found. And that brings to mind a poem I wrote some years ago, it's called RETURNING, so here goes.

Down the road he walked, and there just 'round the bend, stood an ivy covered ruin that was his journey's end.
Thousands of miles he travelled, for something seemed to call, the voices of his ancestors, born within that old stone wall,
As he stands outside that place, now empty and decayed, he looks around at quiet fields, where his forebears worked and played.
From dawn to fall of night, so hard they had to toil, for their food upon the table they depended on the soil.
Then there came a year, when the potato crops all failed, from valley and from mountain the agonised all wailed.

The spectre of starvation cast its shadow across the land, thousands died from hunger, while others lived so grand.
Evicted and burned out, cast on to the side of the road, families torn asunder, dying in the wet and cold.
Ragged covered walking bones, not dead...yet not alive, scavenging the countryside, desperate to survive.
Ireland turned to America in those grief filled years; you threw her out a lifeboat when she was swamped in tears;
Our hard working sons and daughters found refuge on your shore, you gave to them a welcome, and you never closed you doors.

They sailed across the Atlantic, from hunger and from strife, in our darkest hour you were a guiding light.
A real good friend and neighbour, you helped them through the pain, you gave a home and work, restored their pride again.
And there they worked so hard, they shed sweat, tears and blood, they helped to build your railroad across mountain, plain and flood.
They joined your armed forces, fought for the stars and stripes, and when you lost John Kennedy, they cried with you that night.
You took in our emigrants, they proved loyal and true, you gave to them a home, and they gave back to you.

Distinguished sons and daughters, who worked with heart and hand, descendants of those emigrants, became presidents of your land.

And now some are returning to their forebear's native soil, but not in rags and poverty, they return in style.
And lands that once were barren are now bountiful again, but the famines not forgotten here, or the poverty and pain.
And as you walk among us and trod your forebear's sod, we will all remember those who died in field and bog,
America we will remember it was you who gave the call, and said come on I'll help you there's plenty here for all.

JACK: True John, so true, but to paraphrase W B Yeats, all has changed, utterly changed under Trump, a terrible narcissist blowhard has arrived.

JOHN: But how long will he stay! The world looked up to America, but now I get the feeling, America is being laughed at; anyway Jack, as the actress said to the bishop, what's that you have in your hand?

Jack holding some papers in his hand says.

JACK: This is something I wrote on the way over. I'm not saying it's true...but maybe some of it is

JOHN: Get away with ya! You never told the truth in your life! Shure what writer does?

JACK: It's called THERE WERE NO FAST WOMEN ONLY SLOW HORSES.

I like to kid myself that my current losing streak began back in 1973, the year Crisp got mugged in the Grand National by Red Rum. I stood to win a small fortune, having backed him at price at up to 20/1 from Christmas onwards. Instead I lost a small fortune, which increased somewhat when my rented telly sailed through the open window and disintegrated in the back garden shortly after Red Rum passed Crisp yards from the winning post.

In truth, the rot had set in well before then. Probably in 1962, the year Kilmore won the National, and I had a shilling each way at 28/1. Kilmore had been bred and trained in the area before being sold to England, and everyone in the county seemed to know it was going to win.

In hindsight, I should have quit then while I was ahead.

The rot had well and truly taken hold by 1968. By now I had followed Kilmore's hooves to England. The Land of small shovels and big money, as I was led to believe. I fetched up in London, where a stint as a painter at Highbury Stadium convinced the foreman that a dog wagging his tail could do a better job. Still, jobs were ten a penny in those days, and I decided to try my luck as a barman.

Barmen work long hours, but there was always free time in the afternoons – and where better to while away an afternoon than my friendly local bookies? Barry Brogan, David Mould, Ron Hutchinson, I cursed them all – and the three-legged nags they rode when my money was down. And pretty soon not just my money but the pub's as well. It wasn't very difficult to divert some of the takings from the till to my pockets.

The surprise was that they made it so easy for me. One obliging manager even gave me the weekend's takings to bank for him: I got on a bus and didn't stop till I was in Soho!

That became my modus operandi; gain their trust till they let you near the money - and then disappear.

One particular Epsom Derby meeting was very profitable for me. I managed to land a job at the Tattenham Corner House, which overlooked the course, in the week leading up to the Derby. The weather was warm and the punters thirsty, and by the time the meeting was over everyone was knackered. At closing time, the manager decided to dispense with the usual 'reckoning up' of the tills, and to treat the staff to a party instead. And guess who was given the job of locking the tills away in the safe?

I couldn't believe how much money was in that safe. I stuffed bundles in every conceivable carrying place, locked the safe, and then excused myself from the party, feigning a migraine. I then slipped out a side door, walked to the nearest bus stop, and was in central London in less than an hour.

I had fun while the money lasted, but this was tempered by the sense of shock I felt when I was eventually caught and sentenced to eighteen months in goal. It was a salutary lesson, but it didn't stop my gambling. I found it quite easy to gamble in prison; the only difference that the currency was tobacco not money. I soon discovered that losing 'snout' was just as easy as losing money. And when I finished my sentence and was deported, I found my losing streak just as easy to maintain back in Ireland.

John: Christ Jack, for years we have been exporting our young people to England, he must be the first one they sent back.

JACK: Yes John...and in the police car on the way to the plane, Elvis was singing, *return to sender*. Not that he hung around here too long; London was a great place for those with little inclination to get out of bed in the morning, and as the time of the first race usually dictated when I got up, I was soon back there. When I was really desperate, there was always a day's work to be had digging holes for some Irish subby, with cash in your hand at the end of the shift and no questions asked?

Monday mornings were a sight to behold; bleary-eyed and broke we gathered, at the Crown in Cricklewood or the Nags Head in Camden Town, our only trait in common that we were looking for a 'start' – and, more importantly, a sub. In my case, enough to tide me over until the next win came along. With others it was the drink – the 'Diesel'.

MICK: You should have tried the dogs, Jack.

JACK: Well now Mick I did... I did. Hendon, White City, Hackney, I tried them all, and came out poorer but no wiser.

I occasionally bumped into Jack Doyle at the White City, usually with some old 'duchess' on his arm. Jack had come a long way down in the world since his heyday at the same venue, when 90,000 came to see him fight Eddie Philips. And another 100,000 outside, if you believed Jack!

Asked what his downfall was it was always the same reply; 'fast women and slow horses'

JOHN: A fellow gave me a tip onetime; he said it was a sure thing.

MICK: Did you back it?

JOHN: No I didn't, I said thanks very much, but I don't back women or ride horses. Sorry Jack, carry on.

JACK: Park Royal was my favourite dog track. It was there that I almost made my fortune. When I couldn't afford the admission I watched the racing from the roof of a nearby disused factory which overlooked the track, and that was how I discovered that fast starters were seldom caught. A dog a couple of lengths clear at halfway invariably won. I also discovered something else; the commentaries in the nearby betting shop were at least half a minute behind the real thing. Most dog races were nearly over in 30 seconds!

The answer of course was walkie-talkies. My friend – let's call him Larry – and I acquired a couple of these gadgets from a store in Marble Arch and soon the money was rolling in.

Of course not all selections won; but at least half of them did – which was more than enough for us to be rolling in it. I proceeded to give most of it back again to William Hill and Co, until Larry suggested we go in for 'furniture removals'.

It was a brilliant scheme; we invested in a van, Larry inspected empty properties on the pretext of buying them, then we had keys cut. We then proceeded to order furniture and kitchen equipment on the never-never – which we were never-never going to pay for, waited for its delivery, and promptly removed it again. Unfortunately for us, two things happened almost simultaneously: Larry crashed the van and broke his leg in several places, and Park Royal dog track was sold for re-development. End of dream.

MICK: Fair play Jack, you certainly led a colourful life, if only half that is true is it?

JACK: I couldn't possibly comment!

JOHN: I remember Jack Doyle. They say he was a better singer than boxer.

JACK: My mother was a better boxer! He had only one punch, and God help you if he hit you with it. In one fight he threw a haymaker, deliberately missed, and went flying out of the ring. He was counted out sitting on some poor fellas lap. A technical knock-out. The only fighter in history to knock himself out!

JOHN: Another one of De Valera's finest exports who had to cross the water to make a name for himself.

MICK: Of course a lot have emigrated, but I don't think we can blame Pierce and Connelly - or Dev - for that, or for when people over indulge; Pierce and Connolly eventually got what they set out to get, Independence.

JACK: Independence! What Independence? If you think we have, or ever had independence, you're suffering from delusions.1916 was a disorganised skirmish that was an inconvenience to the majority of Dublin citizens and killed many of them. If the English had not executed the leaders it would have been quickly forgotten, that act of execution turned the people of the Country in favour of the revolution. I agree they had a vision of Independence but how it turned out is entirely different.

JOHN: I think you're right Jack. Pearse might be happy enough with the outcome, he got what he wanted, a rosary reciting right wing Catholic country, but I think Connolly is turning in his grave, Connolly was a socialist and his vision of an independent Ireland was not an Ireland run by the Church.

MICK: We are not run by the Church, they might have had a say in something's, but overall we have been run by successive Governments down through the years, since Independence we've had a free and vibrant country.

JOHN: Never free, never vibrant. What the visionaries of 1916 had in mind never came to pass. De Valera handed over the running of the Country to the Catholic church, we got rid of the Monarchy of England and accepted the Monarchy of Rome, and when we threw the shackles of Rome away, we were ensnared by the EU, and every Government since England left, be they Fianna Fail, Fine Gael, or Coalition, has handed the running of the country to Rome first and then the EU, our liberty never got off the ground

JACK: And the Troika walked down O Connell Street, but then we were always used to the Troika here, we've had our own Troika for years, The Catholic church, Fianna Fail, and the GAA. Between them back in the forties, fifties, and sixties, they turned us into a North Korea, brainwashed by afore mentioned Troika; we were living in the teapot and looking out the spout. But then Sean Lemass took over from De Valera and lifted the lid of the teapot and let the light in, and we were enlightened, and it seemed at last after all the years of emigration and poverty, we had arrived.

JOHN: Jobs were created, emigration was down, and prosperity walked every street, road, and boreen. And the GAA lifted the ban on what they referred to as foreign games, a code name for soccer and rugby. Because foreign games weren't banned, American football is more of a foreign game here in Ireland that soccer and rugby ever was, and they allowed that game to be played in Croke Park. So things were looking good, GAA people could attend a soccer or rugby match and not be ostracised in their own parish. The future looked bright... and then we had Charlie, and then Bertie arrived, and with him a return of the Troika, but not a home grown Troika, but a foreign one.

JACK: Bertie Ahern? He was some tulip!

JOHN: Yeah, a tulip, but a rich tulip, digs outs, racehorses, plasters, all and sundry contributing to the good ship Bertie, and for nothing in return...nothing in return my arse.

JACK: He set the ship of state on course for the Iceberg, and no one could deter him from that course.

And when the Iceberg came into view, he jumped ship and handed the controls to Brian Cowen, and the eejit that he was, he took control and the blame for the wreckage, while Bertie sailed away on a lifeboat to count his money in a cupboard.

JOHN: Even Captain Smith, the Captain of the Titanic stayed with his ship.

JACK: Bertie was no Captain Smith, more of an Ishmail, and now leaders of other countries are paying Bertie big money to show them the shortest course to the Iceberg. When he hid in that cupboard, he should have stayed in it.

JOHN: It is indeed a strange world Jack.

MICK: What about his contribution to the peace process?

JOHN: I don't want to go there.

JACK: It stopped the slaughter, but destroyed the political landscape in the North, moderates on all sides of the political spectrum cast aside to placate and put two extremes in control, and not an inch of progress since, no consideration for the North, only for their own existence, that's the legacy of Bertie and Blair.

JOHN: The big difference between the Sunningdale agreement and the Good Friday one... is the fact that Adam's party and Paisley's party weren't the head honchos back then, they said no to everything until they became the two main parties. And then said, yes please

JACK: What were we talking about before? Oh yeah, the GAA ban on playing soccer

MICK: I don't think the ban was taking seriously by some clubs.

JOHN: Well it was taken seriously here, even when the ban was lifted. We had a soccer team here in the seventies, and they organised an Easter raffle for a lamb. They asked the GAA could they make the draw in their little hall in the street, and what do you think the answer was? It was a big fat no... And some of the GAA players playing with the soccer team.

13

JACK: 'Twas even worse down our way. We came out to find our goalposts chopped into pieces in the centre circle one Sunday morning. The local GAA club of course.

JOHN: Local? Where was this?

JACK: Up Limerick way. Kildimo.

JOHN: So you're from stab city eh? I often wondered.

JACK: And now you know! The city of knackers and piebald ponies. I often thought I'd see John Wayne ridin' down O'Connell Street of a Sunday morning there were so many fellas on horseback out and about.

MICK: (imitating John Wayne) Get off ye'r horse and drink yer milk

Maggie goes to the table to pick up empty glasses

MAGGIE: For feck sake, cut out the politics and religion. I thought ye were here to do some reading and sing a few songs.

MICK: We are going to do that Maggie, but you can't have a pub without a row about religion and politics, it's in our DNA.

JOHN: Now, now Maggie, don't get your know what in a twist, I'm going to read a poem now, and then Jack here is going to read a poem or two, or maybe a piece from his book, "Cricklewood Cowboys" or maybe a piece from one of his plays, and then Mick will sing another song.
I was thinking how the world has changed since our time Jack, in our day if a woman left a man, it was for another man, or if a man left a woman it was for another man, but now... now a man might run of with the husband next door, or a woman with the wife next door, so with those thoughts in mind I wrote this poem, it's called She Walked Away

MICK: It is a different world John, gay rights, homosexual, heterosexual, lesbians...

MAGGIE: And a good few has-beens like John there.

JOHN: Ah now Maggie, given the chance I'd still rise to the occasion, anyway listen to this, She walked away.

She was so beautiful, but unavailable to me, she was my world, my land and the sea.
My rivers and valleys and all that is good, and the way that I loved her, no other man could.
To be with her forever was all that I wanted, by her beauty and memory I am still haunted.
When I told her I loved her, she said "that cannot be, I can't love a man, it's a woman for me.
We are friends, and friends we can stay, but my love's for another, and she then walked away.
Walking away to become another woman's wife, and walking beside her, was the rest of my life.

14

Many years have gone by, and I love her still, and I know in my heart that I always will.
She loves another, and I understand, for love is spontaneous, it cannot be planned.
Love is sudden, like a bold from the blue, and when it strikes there's not much you can do.
And a one way love is so hard to bear, and try as you might, you can't make them care.
I'm happy for her if her love is like mine, and the woman she loves is hers for all time.
Time has moved on, I've loved no other, when my bones turn to dust, that dust will love her

MAGGIE: I always knew it John behind that growl there's a soft purr.

Maggie takes out her phone

MAGGIE: Here, let me take a selfie with you, I'll frame it and hang it behind the bar and call it,
The beauty and the beast

JOHN: Ah now Maggie, you're not that bad looking

JACK: Two elderly ladies sitting on a park bench watching a young couple taking a selfie, one old lady says, Bridget what's a selfie? Bridget answers, well when I had a headache, that's what my Henry used to do.

JOHN: Now Jack, what are you going to read?

JACK: That's aisy, John. This is an extract from my play... BRENDAN BEHAN STANDS UP

> *(sings)* Oh a hungry feelin' came oe'r me stealin'
>
> > And the mice were squealin' in my prison cell
> >
> > And the auld triangle went jingle jangle
> >
> > All along the banks of the Royal Canal

That's from The Quare Fella. Do yous know who he was- The Quare Fella? Bernard Canavan was his name. He was in Mount joy jail waiting to be strung up by Pierrepoint for chopping his brother up into little pieces and feeding him to the pigs. Not a very brotherly thing to do was it. Mind you, he was a culchie. Still, I shouldn't complain - it kept me in 'stamps' for a long time.

I love New York. New York is my Lourdes, where I go for spiritual refreshment, a place where you're least likely to be bitten by a wild goat And New York likes Irish people. Not like England. But to be fair to the English, they only dislike some Irish – the same Irish that the Irish themselves dislike, Irish writers. Well, the ones like meself anyway – the ones that think *(more drink)* Well, fuck the begrudgers, that's what I say…

15

Do yous know one British critic asked me? "Mr Behan, what message is in

Your writing? Message", says I. "What the hell do you think I am? A bloody postman!"

Although saying that, Spain takes the biscuit. The only time I ever visited that kip

I was mobbed by a pack of hyenas – well, reporters.

Anyway, one of them asked me what I would most like to see on my visit. Franco's

funeral, says I. Well, before you could say Hiel Hitler, the Fascist bastards threw me

In goal. And then threw me out'a the country

(takes a swig) I saw a sign the other day which said 'Drink Canada Dry'. I'm off there next
week to see if I can manage it.

Ah the Irish God help the Irish, if 'twas raining soup they'd be out there with knives and
forks.

O'Casey once said it was a great place to get a letter from – Ireland I mean. Not if it's from
the fucken taxman!

Dublin is a jealous city. Not a bit like New York. Back there it's hard to find a writer to
admit that a fellow writer can put two words together. Becket was right when he said he'd
rather France at war than Ireland at peace any day of the week.

(listens)

There! Can yous hear Patrick Kavanagh? The Monahan wanker himself! I was goin' up in
the world till I met him. - After that it was downhill all the way.

I told Kavanagh he was *The Last Ploughboy of The Western World.* I mean…you should see
the state of him. Like a bloody orangutang. Spittin' and gobbin' his way through Dublin.
And whinging. Bejasus, if ever there's a begrudgery Olympics in Dublin he'd clear the board
in every event.

Twenty years on he's still sittin' in the corner of McDaids, or wherever, telling people to

either buy him a pint or fuck off. You know the greatest thing he ever wrote? A bloody

cheque that didn't bounce

. *(sings)* On Raglan Road on an autumn day I met her first and knew

  That her dark hair would weave a snare that I would one day rue

That's a song Kavanagh wrote about Hilda Moriarty. The 'love'of his life. Or so he believed.

I bet he never even threaded her…But let me tell you sumthin' for nothin' - there's plenty
that did

16

I had the pleasure of Hilda's company last year. Down in Limerick, the capital of culchieland. I think it was the monsoon season down there...Anyway, there I was, drying meself off in the bar of Dooley's Hotel, when over she comes. The belle of every ball in Dublin!

I heard Paddy followed you to Dingle for the Christmas last year, I said to her, and you never even gave him a turkey sandwich.

He wasn't invited, she said.

I thought you were his mot, says I.

I was never his...mot, as you so elegantly put it, she replied.

Well, you live and learn. Anyway, what she wanted was for me to lay off Paddy. He hasn't been well lately, she said

Sure, he hasn't been well all his life! He's a fucken head case. And besides, he can fight his own battles. Kavanagh's a culchie. And I hate all culchies.

Then she accused me of throwing him into the Royal canal.

Not guilty, your honor.

But someone did throw him in.

Oh, they did that. Bejasus they did! Head-first!

You want suspects? How about half of Dublin.

No, I didn't throw him in – but I'll tell you wha - I'd like to get hold of the bollix that pulled him out.

(*sings*)Oh the wind that blows across the fields from Mucker

      Brings a perfume that the city does not know

      And the culchie in McDaids that's drinking porter

      Spakes a language that we townies do not know

Anyway, Kavanagh wasn't good enough for Hilda. A doctor's daughter, studying

Medicine at UCD, and he a small farmer studying droppings on a dunghill. How

could she take that yoke to mama and papa? He had a face like a horse. Not that she

Was short of other suiters. A little while later she married Donncha O'Malley. Thanks

be to jaysus she had some bit of sense anyway. Mind you, he was another culchie...

      Oh stony grey soil of Monaghan.

The laugh from my loved you thieved.

You took the gay child of my passion

And gave me your clod-conceived

Clod conceived!

If he loved his stony grey soil so much why didn't he fucken stay there. And save us all a fortune

....

JOHN: I think Kavanagh was a better writer than Behan, well a better poet anyway, Raglan Road, a Christmas Carol, Oh Stony Grey Soil, The Great Hunger, all fantastic poems. Kavanagh was a wordsmith, and Behan, a brawlin' bowsies, was jealous of him, I know Kavanagh was cantankerous and bummed drink off his friends, but he was a great poet.

MICK: No doubt Behan was jealous of Kavanagh; Jack just said it in his play, what was it you said Jack?

JACK: Dublin is a jealous City; it's hard to find a writer to admit that a fellow writer could put two words together.

MICK: I suppose that's true some writers would rather heap praise on a dogs shit on the road than praise a fellow writer, so we can also say Kavanagh was jealous of Behan, but I'll say one thing, Jack is bringing Behan's brawling, bruising vulgarity, and his innocence to life in that play, continue Jack.

JACK: *(sings)*

On the eighteenth day of November

Outside the town of Macroom

The Tans in the big Crossley tender

Were driving along to their doom

But the boys of the brigade were waiting

With hand grenades primed on the spot

And The Irish Republican Army

Made shite of the whole fucken' lot

Aren't the Brits wonderful itself? First they put me in jail and then they made me a rich man

I done me porridge in England. And what for? I didn't get very far in Liverpool, did I? All I was going to do was stick a few Peggy's Legs down the funnel of a battleship in the docks and pretend it was Guy Fawkes Night. The peelers nabbed me before I even left me room. Three years Borstal. I went in a boy and came out a man. And an atheist to boot.

They said that the ruination of my country has been caused by our over-fondness for drink. As a nation, I mean. I can think of many things that caused the ruination of our country – and they had fuck-all to do with the gargle. Cromwell, The Penal Laws, Partition, to name but a few.

'To Hell or to Connaught'. That was Cromwell's advice to all Irish Catholics.

> *"Under penalty of death, no Irish man, woman, or child, is*
> *to let himself, herself, itself be found east of the River Shannon after May 1st 1654'*

Ah yes, a very civilized nation the English were back then. Not that they had improved much by 1916 – or 1946

Any country that can send a gunboat up the Liffey, to defeat six hundred men, when she already has thirty thousand soldiers pounding the bejaysus out'a them, can't call it cricket. With a few more guns ourselves we'd have riveted a lot more of their brave boys to the railings around O'Connell Street.

Did I not tell yous I was in the IRA? The Dublin Brigade. The elite of the Irish Republican Army. We might not have fancy guns and uniforms, but Bejasus we wiped the smiles off a lot of faces with what we did have. The ould conjurer's trick of potash, chloride and sulphuric acid worked wonders…

  Then I had that bit of bother in Glasnevin and I lost touch for with real life for another few years. It was my jailing for the attempted murder of a Special Branch man in Glasnevin cemetery during the Easter Rising commemoration service.
I did fire a couple of shots at the Special Branchers, but jaysus, they were firin' at me! I went on the run, but me own side weren't too happy. I'd taken the gun with me you see – IRA property – and I heard that they sentenced me to death in me absence. I sent them a nice letter asking them could they carry out the sentence in me absence too!

Ah, it all blew over eventually.

(sings)   All round my hat I will wear a three-colour-ribbon-oh

         All round my hat till death comes to me.

         And if anyone asks me why I do wear it

         I will say for my true love whom I ne'er more shall see.

An' as for the oul' religion. My ould fella wouldn't be seen dead inside a church. But he'd call us every Sunday morning; '*Go out and meet your God you lazy pack of hounds*'

Once a priest called to get up a collection for the Fascists in Spain – and we starvin' with the cold and hunger ourselves. Da fucked him off and the priest told him we'd burn in hell for eternity. *'At least we'll be fucking warm'*, Da shouted.

All that talk about damnation. We were damned all right – like all the poor in this country. Damned with hunger.

Prayer and masturbation. The Catholic Church's answer to promiscuity. Well, they're fifty percent right. Sex and religion, that's what has Ireland banjaxed, not enough of the first and too much of the other or is it the other way round? Ma, now, she had no interest in sex. All she did was lie back and count the pawn tickets.

During my *Borstal Boy* days the prison chaplain wouldn't let me attend Mass if I didn't renounce the IRA. I told him to fuck off. Wasn't I in good company? Weren't the rebels in '98 excommunicated, wasn't De Valera and ten thousand others ex-communicated in 1922 - me own father included?

The Bishops of Ireland would ex-communicate their own mothers, given the chance - the poxy fucken' druids.

(sings) Never throw stones at your mother

      You'll be sorry when she's dead

      Never throw stones at your mother

      Throw bricks at your father instead...

(Takes a swig from his bottle) Up the Republic! Up…my arse. D'you know something? I have no politics. I make them up as I go along. Communism, Socialism, and Rheumatism - they're all the fucking same... *(Swigs again)* Up Dev!

Ah yes, De Valera, the fucken Spaniard. I spent four years in the Curragh at his pleasure.

The scrawny bastard. It was because of him we were neutral in the war. Where England

is concerned, Ireland can never be neutral. You're either for them or against them.

Dev should have contacted his friend Mr Hitler and asked to borrow a couple of his

Doodlebugs. Then a couple of us could have dropped them on the House Of Commons

under the cover of darkness and blown the shaggin lot to kingdom come.

They say De Valera fought against the English. But he fought against his own people too. Should we praise him for that? Brother against brother, father against son. Ireland lost some of her finest sons in that little disagreement.

(sings) 'Twas on an August morning, all in the morning hours

I went to take the morning air all in the month of flowers

And there I saw a maiden and heard her mournful cry

'Oh, what will mend my broken heart, I've lost my laughing boy'.

Now Michael Collins. He was the flower of the flock. No doubt about that. Do you know what, instead of executing Pierce, Connolly and the rest of them they should have charged them with disturbing the peace and given them seven days, and that would have been the end of the republican movement…

MICK: That's mighty stuff Jack, and was that play staged in London?

JACK: It was and went down very well - and had some of Behan's relations in the audience. Right Mick, let's hear another song, what are you going to sing?

MICK: The one John wrote about an old fellow being a stranger in his own village.

JACK: An old fellow can be a stranger in a city as well as a village...

JOHN: Begod don't I know it! This is called, "Drinkin' with Ghosts"

Mick sings.

He sat at the bar, he was drinkin' some beer / a vacant seat near him, I asked, can I sit here?
Hr turned around, and then said to me / if you sit there you'll sit on her knee.

Chorus

I'm drinkin' with ghosts tonight, I'm drinkin' with ghosts, my old friends are here / some drinkin' whiskey, some drinkin' beer.
I'm drinkin' with ghost, I'm waltzing with shadows / I'm lying on a beach, I'm running through meadows.
She's right beside me, the love of my life / I'm drinkin' with ghosts tonight.

He said if you look around, all your friends you can see / all my friends are gone, there's only just me.
I'm a blast from the past, from along ago time / and the world that you live in is different to mine.

Repeat Chorus

He got of his seat, and walked to the door / I thought I saw shadows waltz 'cross the floor,
He said, I'll just open this door and step on to the street / it's time now to go / I have old friends to meet.

Repeat chorus, and add to the end. Drinkin' with ghosts, waltzing with shadows, I'm meting my friends tonight.

JACK: Follow that, says the fella!

JOHN: I'll read a piece from my book DUST COVERED MEMORIES. A piece about youth and old age, now let's see where to start? Ah yes here we go, this piece, Ted is reminiscing about his youth to his young friend Jim.

Do you want tea or coffee Jim?
I'll have coffee.
You stay here, it's such a lovely morning I'll make the coffee and bring it out.
I sat there waiting for Ted, hearing nothing only the sound of nature. I was reminded of a couple of lines of a poem I read somewhere, *season of colourful flowers and happy hearts, dancing singing and seaside play / birds and bees, and other summer sounds form a choir to sing you through the day.*
Just as Ted came with the coffee, a young couple, about nineteen or twenty passed on their way to the sea.

Ted said, how I envy them. To be that age again if only for one glorious day, to be young and free again. To be in love, to be in Tramore on a summer's evening having fun on the bumpers and hurdy-gurdys, to listen to Brendan Boyer singing *Kiss Me Quick*. To eat chips from vinegar soaked brown bag
To walk from the Atlantic Ballroom with the one of your dreams and admire a full moon casting a shimmering silver streak of light on the surface of the sea. To experience once more what it's like to be in love, and to be loved, and then spend a restless night in anticipation of another day. No need to die to go to heaven, what could be more heavenly than a summer's day with the one you love.

Young girl in a summer dress / her lovely face the sun caress,
Nimble of limb she walks by / I watch her pass, I heave a sigh,
Recalling days that used to be / alas those days no more for me.

Days of youth, days of bliss / days of love and tender kiss,
Those teenage years full of joy / and first love for girl and boy,
Nights of love, dance and song / those carefree days now all gone.

Gone...gone, gone forever, memories where would we be without them.
Ted handed me the coffee.
I asked, is that poem a lament for the past Ted.
It's for the past and the present, the first line in John Keats poem "Endymion, *is a thing of beauty is a joy forever.*
And so it should be Ted.
 It should be, but it's not.
What do you mean; surely you can enjoy any form of beauty you like.

You would think so, but I'm only allowed to enjoy some forms of beauty. Young and old can gaze upon and admire the beauty of a sunset or sunrise, young and old can gaze upon and admire a sunlit grove of bluebells, or the golden sheen of furze on a hillside, young and old can admire a beautiful work of art, or an old, or new piece of architecture. But if a young lady walks by, only the young are allowed to gaze, if an old man admires her beauty, he is deemed a pervert. The world does not seem to understand that the ability to appreciate all forms of beauty does not deteriorate with old age.

Interval if required
Act 2

MICK: Maggie, come out from behind that counter and let John admire you.

MAGGIE: I'd love to Mick, but I can't take a chance, someone might say we have pervert on the premises and call the guards.

MICK: Or, he might collapse and we'd have to call an ambulance.

JOHN: As the Queen said to Prince Phillip when she saw what was on offer, "We are not amused"

JACK: I was just thinking the other day; we've just finished celebrating the anniversary of 1916, and soon we'll be preparing for the anniversary of the civil war.

MICK: I hope they don't look at it through rose tinted glasses like they did with 1916; the civil war anniversary will be complicated, for the truth was never told

JOHN: It's going to be hard to placate the two civil war parties, a lot of questions to be answered, for instance why was it started? Why we were never taught anything about it in national school in the forties and fifties?

JACK: It will take a brave politician to answer your first question Mick; I'll answer the second one myself. The gombeen men ruled. Fianna Fail were in power for most of the forties and fifties, and of course that meant a Fianna Fail Minister for education, it would take a brave teacher even to mention the Civil War, never mind discuss it, remember this was a time in Ireland when the Government and the Catholic Church were sacking female teachers who became pregnant out of wedlock.

Maggie shouts at John from behind counter.

MAGGIE John I heard a lovely poem of yours last Sunday night on John O' Shea's programme on WLR, It's called "Make Love Not War" and since ye are blabbing on about war, would you read it for us?

JOHN: Ah, Maggie, I didn't know you cared, I'd make love to you anytime... so just for you, here's "Make Love, Not War."

Make love not war and the world will be a better place to live, maybe a sign of peace and harmony is what we all should give.
This world is oh...so small, when compared to the universe for size, but we must learn to share it, rich and poor, the foolish and the wise.
All Christians, Jews, and Muslims, believe their god is right, and then they try to prove it with mayhem, death, and might.
You are right to revere your God, and to believe that he's the best, but you have no right to force that belief on me and all the rest.
I believe our God's are peaceful, but we put those God's to shame, when we cause death and carnage, and we cause it in their name.
I'm sure you must have noticed as they gather up the dead, the victims... though of different creed and colour, all their blood ran red.
And whatever is your colour, whether it's yellow, white or black, your skin is just the wrapping, and you cannot give it back.

If I could find a peace dust, I'd climb a mountain high, and there I'd cast it to the wind and stand and watch it fly.
And as it blew around the world, it would bring wars to an end, spreading peace and harmony and turning foe to friend.
But I cannot find a peace dust; I know that's just a dream, so peace and understanding must come by other means.
Are our God's that different? Or is us the human race? Who cannot accept each other's, politics, creed and face?
What if I told you; our God's are from the same large tree, and sprouting from the one root, a branch for you and me.
So make love not war and the world will be a better place to live, maybe a sign of peace and harmony is what we all should give.
This world is oh...so small when compared to the universe for size, but we must learn to share it, rich and poor, the foolish and the wise.

JACK: That's powerful, John. Are you sure you're not related to Bob Dylan?

JOHN: No Jack, but I'll soon be a Zimmerman, when they give me a Zimmer frame, read one of your poems, or something from "Cricklewood Cowboys."

JACK: Follow that, he says! This is a piece about The Royal Dukes. Who remembers them? No one, I expect

MICK: Go way or that, Jack! Seamie Brien, P J Kirwan, yerself...the Portlaw boys. Ireland's answer to The Beatles!

JACK: Ah stop it now, Mick! (he reads)

For my eighteenth birthday I got a union card, a crash helmet and the news that I was to start shift work in the rubber department in the Tannery. The rubber department was as different from the leather-board shop as a milking parlour from a bakery. Rows of machines lined the floor, looking, for all the world, like something out of a Marvel comic, their short, squat bodies festooned with pulleys and handles.

In here, shoe-soles of all shapes and sizes were turned out in their thousands. Bales of rubber were brought in, cut into thin slabs then delivered in bins to the machine operators. The slabs were then placed in the moulds and the machines set in motion. When the moulding process was complete, the moulds were emptied, and the filled bins carted away for despatch to some English shoe manufacturer.

The union card was compulsory on reaching the age of eighteen. For the payment of a shilling a week you got the privilege of voting in the shop-steward election once a year, and going on strike with no union pay when a dispute had to be settled.

The crash helmet wasn't compulsory, but mother said I should wear it all the same. I did so when I remembered.

On the music front, a new era had begun. The Beatles, The Rolling Stones had broken new ground, were changing all the rules, and we wanted to be part of it. Gone were the staid and strait-laced days of the foxtrot and the waltz; new dances were springing up all over the world; fashion was becoming outlandish and outrageous; Mods and Rockers were fighting over girls in Brighton and Clacton, Beatle-mania was sweeping the world. We wanted to be part of the revolution.

There was no apartheid in the rubber department; girls as well as boys operated the machines, and it was clear that they, too, wanted to break the mould. Bee-hive hair-dos' appeared, skirts began to creep upward, and it slowly dawned on us that girls did have legs above their knees.

It was no secret that we were trying to put a band together. And when Paul Gorman confessed that he, too, was trying to do the same, the germ of an idea was born. Why didn't we join forces? Kilmac and Portlaw come together in some venture? It couldn't work, would it? The only time they came together was on the sports field – when they usually kicked the shite out of each other.

Our first meetings were exploratory, but they turned out more productive than we expected; We all wanted a band with a brass section, and when we found that Paul played the saxophone and David Hallissey the trumpet...well, that was the brass section taken care of. The next problem was the drummer; they had Brendan O'Shea and we had PJ. Then we saw Brendan perform on the drums and that was the drummer problem solved. That meant me becoming the bass guitarist and PJ the rhythm guitarist. Neither of us minded too much; I had been experimenting with the bass already and PJ was already an accomplished guitar player. That only left Tony Regan. What could he play? After some discussion we decided we would buy a trombone and he could learn to play it.

Seamie solved the problem of where to rehearse with our now-expanded group. Michael Baron, the owner of the Rainbow Hall, also owned a joinery firm and Seamie worked for him. When he heard of our predicament, he offered us the use of the Rainbow on the nights it wasn't in use, usually Tuesday and Thursday nights.

The name was less easy. Many were thought up and discarded. The Young Ones, The Young Devils. However, when the parish priest heard this last name being mentioned he came to see us and told us to find something more fitting. The Young Shadows was one we all liked but there was a group in Dublin already called that. The name 'Royal' was very popular with bands, and when someone came up with the word 'Duke', we thought it had a certain ring to it. We became The Royal Dukes.

Practice was hard work – especially for those not too acquainted with their instruments. I didn't have much of an ear for music- tone deaf would be putting it mildly – so my bass notes depended on what chords Seamie was playing at any given time. This meant keeping one eye on his fingers, and one on my own playing - a practice from which anybody watching would conclude that I was cross-eyed. Then we discovered a sheet-music shop in Dungarvan. Buying the sheets at least stopped me from developing a squint, for, although I couldn't read music, the guitar chords were clearly indicated.

We also needed microphones and amplifiers, and here Pat Barron, Michael's brother, helped out. Pat was lead guitarist with the Pat Irwin band and he passed us on some amplification they no longer used.

Listening to ourselves in those early days was painful. We recorded some of our efforts and then played them back. One of the first was' Send Me The Pillow That You Dreamed On', a song made popular by Johnny Tillotson. We murdered it; off note, off key, out of tune, out of time, you name it, we did it. We played it back a second time; it sounded even worse. Seamie was tearing his hair out; *never mind the same key, boys, could we all try and play the same tune!*

Gradually we got better. Slowly, the realisation dawned that we were beginning to sound like a coherent unit. A band that now needed an audience, for a band that merely played behind closed doors was as useful as a car without wheels.

Michael Barron proved to be our saviour once again. He booked us as relief band at a forthcoming dance at The Rainbow. The date was a couple of months off so we had plenty of time for preparation. Or so we thought. We weren't half ready. We never would be. We had to get jackets made, learn a dance routine, get ourselves better equipment. And Tony must learn to play his trombone. He couldn't blow a note yet.

Slowly but surely the problems sorted themselves out. We went to a tailor in Dungarvan and he measured us up for our new jackets. We choose a broad blue-and-grey striped material, and picked a design similar to that worn by the Beatle. We worked on the dance routine, and found a supplier of hired amplification equipment in Town.

That only left Tony and his trombone. By now it was abundantly clear that he would never play the trombone. His best efforts so far had resembled a couple of jackasses bawling in unison. In the end we decided he should mime playing his instrument. This he did, moving with the rest of us in the dance routines, blowing silent notes on the trombone. It worked a treat; who was going to know what a trombone sounded anyhow with a saxophone and a trumpet blasting away?

The big night drew ever nearer. Posters had gone up all over the locality; RAINBOW HALL, SUNDAY. Music by the DAVITT BROTHERS. Supported by new local sensations THE ROYAL DUKES. This was heady stuff, and every time I passed a poster I stopped to read it – just to convince myself I wasn't dreaming.

There was still no sign of our jackets. All sort of excuses were trotted out; the material had to come from England, the machinist had flu, the buttons hadn't yet arrived. We intensified our practicing. As soon as a new song appeared we rushed out to get the sheet music. 'It's Been A Hard Day's Night' was rehearsed over and over, trying to capture some of the essence of the Beatles sound. But it was' I Can Get No Satisfaction' that was our trump card. Tum-tum –ta-ta –da-da-da –da –tum-tum...I practiced the bass notes incessantly. 'I can get no – sat-is-fac-tion,' sang Seamie in reply.

The song was causing much rage throughout the establishment. Radio Eireann was refusing to play it; the parish priest condemned it from the pulpit, but the youngsters were glued to their transistors, listening to it on Radio Luxemburg. Fr. Sinnott came to our rehearsals and heard us play it. The devil's music, he called it, and said it was a mortal sin.

What...like adultery or murder? My soul could be forever damned for singing a song? I doubted it, somehow. By now my relationship with the church was changing. Gone were my altar-boy fancies for the priesthood, gone my implicit belief in the all-embracing goodness of the Catholic Church. I had now read up on historical events like the Crusades and the Spanish Inquisition – where people were imprisoned, tortured and burnt at the stake, all in the name of religion. It didn't seem like a particularly religious activity to me. Oh, I still went to Mass on a Sunday, but that was only because it was expected and not because I wanted to. What sort of hypocrisy was that? I had begun to question our fundamental beliefs; The Holy Trinity, The Virgin Mary, the infallibility of the Pope, even the story of Adam and Eve. If the latter was true then Cain must have committed incest, mustn't he?

I felt anger about the priest's visit to our rehearsals; what right had he to tell us what music we could play. Later that night I wrote some verse about it.

Son, the priest said, put that guitar away

And get your hair cut, right

And don't play I Can Get No Satisfaction

Tonight

It's a sin to call yourselves

The Red Devils, he said

And in the distance

I could see mother nodding her head

So we became The Royal Dukes

And played Nineteenth Nervous Breakdown instead

Saturday came and no jackets. We were resigned to appearing jacket-less. White shirts and dark pants would have to do.

Shortly after six on Sunday we all met up in the Rainbow to set up our equipment before the Davitt Brothers arrived. Seamie came direct from Town, having picked up the amplifiers and other bits and pieces. He also brought seven jackets. The tailor had brought them round to his house earlier that day.

Christ, they were beautiful, those jackets. You could die happy in them. There was an old full-length mirror backstage and we strutted about in front of this for ages, admiring ourselves from every angle. Eventually, we reluctantly took them off and got on with setting up our gear.

The Rainbow was bursting at the seams that night. Curiosity, I suppose. The Davitt Brothers seemed bemused by it all. They were a competent outfit who had been playing the country venues for a number of years, and were used to sedate Macra Na Feirme and Muintir Na Tire supporters; nothing like the high excitement that was in evidence here. As the dance began and we listened to them play, we realised how much better than us they sounded.

It didn't seem to matter. As they took their break and we replaced them. The crowd went wild. You would think we were The Beatles; they solidified into one heaving mass, packing the dance area. It was obvious there would be no dancing; they only wanted to listen and watch.

Looking out into the sea of faces I could see many I recognised; Jim Kiersey, his black hair slicked back, a crease on one side that would split timber; Vince Power, giving me the thumbs up; Shirley Mulcahy, on shoes so high she must have used a step-ladder; Tony Casey, Elvis quiff dripping oil. I closed my eyes briefly and said a prayer.

I needn't have worried. We could have banged tin cans together and they would have cheered. 'I Can Get No Satisfaction' was our opening number and it nearly brought the house down. After that it was plain sailing; a few Beatles numbers, Jim Reeves, Jumbalaya, You Ain't Nuthin' But A Hound-Dog. Paul did a bit of Yakety –Sax, Seamie did 'Apache'. We closed with Tony singing 'Take These Chains From My Heart.'

Or thought we did. They wouldn't let us finish. We had to run through several of the songs again. It was almost an hour before the Davitts came back on stage again. The Royal Dukes were in business!

JOHN: Now we're motorin' lads! Seamie would have been here tonight – if he wasn't otherwise engaged. Come on Mick, another song.

Mick: I'll sing the one you gave me to put a tune to "Permanent Tear" although I don't think it will cheer us up Jack, it's about some girl he met at a fair in Hampstead, and then she walked out on him.

JOHN: She never lived with me to walk out.

MICK: Here we go.

In the morning when waking, my heart is breaking; I realize I'm all alone; I am so lonely, there's just me only ever since you left our home.
My heart is broken, so I go to my local, and I'm drinking whiskey and beer, my friends they come by and each of them try to dry up this permanent tear.
The band is playing, the dancers are swaying, but I don't hear them at all, 'because you're not here, and without you my dear, I could never walk tall.
I pick up my phone, I call her home, her mother says, she is not here, she has left you, she's found someone new, once more that permanent tear'

Chorus

I've got a tear, a permanent tear ever since you said good bye, I've got a tear a permanent always that tear in my eye.
To me you were so good, without you I'm no good, why did you go way? Now that you're gone it's hard to go on, how can I get through the day?

I go to my bed, I lay down my head, but I can't get any sleep, I stare at the ceiling, such a sad feeling, once more I'm starting to weep.
The nights are much colder and I long to hold her, and oh how I wish she was here, and God knows I miss her and I long to kiss her and dry up this permanent tear.
Outside it's raining; inside I'm paining as I wonder where it went wrong, my mind says let go, my hearts saying no, it won't accept she has gone.
It just won't believe it that she would deceive it, and throw away all of those years, but it's no use pretending, there's no happy ending; I must live with this permanent tear.

Chorus

JACK: Great, great Mick, she must have a left a bit of an impression on you John.

JOHN: Young love Jack, so important one day, and forgotten the next, not like our civil War, still not forgotten and hundredth anniversary coming up shortly I wonder what way will they commemorate?

Jack: What way will they commemorate the civil war? It's going to be awkward for whoever is in power... I often wonder what kind of a country we would have had if the civil war never started, if De Valera had accepted like the majority of the people did what Collin's brought back? And remember what Collins brought back was just a stepping stone, and if accepted, maybe with ongoing negotiations we could have got thirty two counties

MICK: De Valera was right not to accept it, he wanted a thirty two county Republic, and he was willing to fight for it.

JOHN: He was willing to fight for it, and he did, but was he fighting for a Republic or for his own survival, remember when the people accepted in an election what Collins brought back...De Valera was yesterdays man, and the big question, why didn't De Valera go to England himself?

JACK: De Valera didn't go to England, because he was of the opinion that nothing was to be gained, and Collin's would return empty handed, remember, Collins at this point in time was the man of the people, De Valera was becoming insignificant, he needed to regain his popularity, he hoped the people would look upon Collin's as a failure.

MICK: Nonsense, he wanted thirty two counties, and he was willing to do all he could to get it.

JOHN: If that is so Mick, why when he eventually came to power, and remember he ran this country for almost fifty years, why for that fifty years did he abandon the North and left the nationalists at the mercy of the unionists, to be treated as dirt in their own country?

JOHN: Anyway lads, let's get back to the poetry, music and song. Have you anything left, Jack?

JACK: As the actress said to the archbishop. How about this, It's a chapter from CRICKLEWOOD COWBOYS. And a girl called Tessa

'Meet Tessa - my new partner', said Chris as I entered the living room.

'I already have', I shouted. 'She stole my bloody wallet'.

It was barely an hour since our first meeting. The venue had been the Banba Club, at the tea-dance, where hung-over Irishmen sobered up on a Sunday afternoon, waiting for the pubs to re-open. Situated up an alleyway off the Kilburn High Road, it was a low-roofed shack of a building, and had probably once seen service as stables. Some of the locals were of the opinion that it still catered for animals.

The afternoon had been a little more eventful than usual; apart from the removal of my wallet and the mandatory couple of fights, The Sunshine Gang had paid one of their occasional visits. They had, as usual, been repelled. But not before they had wedged a Mini in the entrance, busted a doorman's nose, and smashed the window to the ticket office. In the fighting that had ensued, sheer numbers had driven them back into the street. They had retreated, vowing revenge. I had landed a punch on a greasy head and had returned to the mineral bar feeling pleased with myself.

The dance that followed was a Siege of Ennis, and I found myself dragged into the mass of gyrating bodies by Tessa. She stood out among the other dancers; tall and athletic- looking, ash-blonde hair billowing out behind her as she jigged - inexpertly - to the music. I managed to hang on to her for the following slow waltz, and discovered that it was her first time to an Irish dance. Afterwards, she disappeared to wherever it is women go to when dances are over. A few minutes later I discovered my wallet had disappeared too.

'No hard feeling, Terry?' She handed me back the wallet, a big grin on her face. 'It wasn't my idea'.

'I know it wasn't'. I extracted a fiver and handed it to Chris. 'You proved your point'.

'I told you she was good'. He laughed and clapped me on the back.

Chris' pick -and-shovel days were over. His weekly ten-shilling accumulator on the ITV Seven had finally come good: from his winnings he had purchased a new suit and shoes, and became a pickpocket in the West End. Tessa was his latest assistant.

Tessa lit up a cigarette then offered them round. 'Is that what you call a dance in Ireland?

Chris laughed. 'It was a bit lively, I suppose'.

'Who, exactly, is The Sunshine Gang?' she asked

Larry raised his head from The Sporting Chronicle. 'A bunch of bowsies from back yonder'. Where yonder was he didn't specify. 'We had the right treatment for them in Ringsend'.

'We Know. The ould Ringsend uppercut', I chuckled, having heard it all before.

'And what is a Ringsend uppercut?' she asked

'A good kick in the…' Larry hesitated, 'what's-its'.

Chris nudged Tessa. 'Larry used to run with them, didn't you?'

'From a distance, boy. Only from a distance'. He snorted. 'They came over here to lick their wounds'.

Despite Larry's low opinion of them, they had already acquired a reputation in the area, and when fights broke out in the dancehalls and clubs they were usually in the thick of it.

The arrival of Tessa changed our lives quite a lot. I had never met anyone quite like her before. She wasn't the first liberated woman I had come in to contact with, but she was different. Certainly different from the Irish girls you met at the dances in the Galtymore and the 32 Club. Oh, you could shift them, but no matter how much drink you poured down their gullets, all you were likely to get at the end of the night was a good feel. And sometimes not even that. Getting your leg over meant putting a roof over their heads. Marriages might be made in heaven but they were negotiated in dancehalls like the Galtymore.

They worked like beavers in the sweatshops of Kilburn and Cricklewood. At Smiths and Walls, Heinz and Unigate, from eight till five, then hurried away to supplement their meagre wages by doing evening shifts as usherettes and assemblers in the cinemas and factories. Weekends they prowled the dancehalls looking for husbands - men who would be content with a furtive fumble in the back of a Mini or Austin 1100, and who could be weaned off the Guinness without too much fuss. Oh yes, behind every drunken Irishman was a sober Irish girl.

Into this came Tessa like a breath of fresh air. Twiggy, Jean Shrimpton, songs of peace, rioting students, she scorned all that. She was a materialist, out, as she put it, to screw the world before it screwed her. There was no such thing as free love.

'There's a price for everything', she said, 'especially love'.

'Why a pickpocket?' I asked her one evening.

'Why not? It's better than a bleedin' factory. I left school at fifteen, home at sixteen. I got cheesed off being pawed by my dad - step-dad actually - and my mum couldn't give a toss. Too busy doing the amusement arcades by day and her bingo at night. My brother Ben was nicking cars for a living - when he wasn't inside. I just took off one day. I don't think anybody missed me'.

One afternoon she turned up at the flat, limping. She asked me to fetch some ice-cubes, and then explained she had fallen down some steps on the Embankment.

'Stupid, really. I wasn't watching where I was going and tripped over. I had the stuff Chris passed to me in my bag. It could have been serious, I guess…'

'Maybe it's an omen'.

She laughed. 'If you believe all that crap. My mum believes in black cats, not walking under ladders, throwing salt over your left shoulder, all that stuff, and it hasn't brought her much luck. I believe you make your own'.

Her skirt had ridden up and I could see her knickers. Black, lacy affairs. Go on, something kept telling me, she wouldn't let you see the view if she didn't want you to do something about it. However, before I could act, the door opened and Chris walked in.

My drift into crime probably began with that incident, because next day I was standing in for her as Chris's assistant. And very boring it was too. I spent my time sauntering up and down a stretch of Piccadilly while he searched for suitable victims. At the end of the day we had acquired a purse with everything in it except money, a wallet containing five one pound notes, a train ticket to Hemel Hempstead, and a photo of a nude woman with 'I love you, Dicko' scrawled across it. Our other acquisition confirmed my suspicions that the English were sex-mad; a gold-embossed cigarette case with ten French ticklers packed neatly inside. We shared the condoms and pawned the case for eight quid. Not exactly a fortune for a day's work. Chris said there were better days, but I didn't really fancy it. I was glad when Tessa recovered.

Since Jonjo's death I hadn't taken a pick or shovel in my hand. And I had no intention of doing so. London was a goldmine, waiting to be exploited. Larry was right; it was a great place for those with no intention of getting up in the morning. We began stealing on a small scale, and found the Portobello market on a Saturday morning very obliging. It was incredibly easy; hiding the gear in special pockets inside our long coats. Jeans and shirts were the easiest to flog in the pubs we hawked them round. We extended our operations to take in other markets; Petticoat Lane and Brick Lane, and found that shops like Burtons and Colliers were just as obliging.

By now I had acquired Larry's passion for the horses. Sometimes it seemed as if I was stealing for William Hills or Terry Downes; come late afternoon, the money I'd made in the morning had vanished behind the counter of a dingy betting shop in Willesden Lane or Kilburn High Road. Other times we were rolling in it; like when Saucy Kit won the Champion Hurdle and Fleet the One Thousand Guineas, and we had them doubled up to win hundreds of pounds. We followed up on Royal Palace in the Two Thousand Guineas and The Derby.

It was Tessa who suggested the break in Brighton when she saw us counting our winnings after the Derby. Larry wouldn't come - he had bought a small van for fifty pounds and wanted to practice his driving - so Chris, Tessa and myself headed off.

I still couldn't figure Tessa out. For several months now she had graced us with her presence, but she was as enigmatic as ever. One thing was clear though; she wasn't Chris's girlfriend, merely his working partner. She was even vague about where she lived; over Walthamstow way was the nearest I could pin her down to, and if Chris knew he wasn't saying. Sometimes we wouldn't see her for a week or more, and apart from occasional outingsto the pub with us, where she downed pints of lager without ever seeming to get pissed; her social life was a total mystery. I badly wanted to get inside her knickers, and it was frustrating watching her parade her talents round the flat when I couldn't seem to get close to her.

Brighton changed all that. We were like kids again at the seaside. We built sandcastles, raced each other along the beach, and got sick on jellied eels. And even sicker on beer. We had taken sleeping bags with us, sleeping huddled together beneath the promenade for the first few nights. Then Chris met an old friend, and she dragged him off to the Isle of Wight to some concert she had tickets for. I was fed up of sleeping on lumpy terrain, so I suggested we book into a couple of hotel rooms that night.

.'Make it a double', she replied.

Making love with her was like being aboard a runaway train. A hair-raising ride, constantly picking up speed, gathering momentum. I wondered if we were ever going to stop. On and on we rode, free-wheeling in places, generating sparks galore where the friction was fiercest. Eventually, we coasted to a stop on an uphill section. Out of steam. Well, I was anyway. Her body in repose was the nearest thing to a work of art I had ever seen. Long flanks perfectly aligned, breasts sculpted out of the finest, palest clay; nostrils flared, lips slightly parted as

35

she slumbered.

Sunrise found us on the beach again, watching the sun clamber over the horizon. I knew how it felt.

It was then that she asked me for a hundred pounds.

'It's for my mum. To stop the bailiffs givin' her the heave-ho. Dad's done a runner again and Ben's in the nick…'

'It's a lot of dosh, I said'.

She shrugged. 'It's only money, Terry. Bits of paper. Easy come, easy go. Besides, you'll only lose it all again. You always do'. She rubbed a hand along the inside of my thigh. 'Think of it as a long-term investment'.

I couldn't figure out what she was offering me; love, friendship, or merely the use of her body. Whatever it was, I wanted it. I gave her the hundred quid. When we got back to London Bridge she kissed me goodbye and said she would see me soon.

'Where's Tessa?' Larry asked when he saw me on my own.

'You guess is as good as mine. She borrowed some money then took off'.

He looked at me in a peculiar fashion. 'She borrowed some off me too. Before ye left. For her brother's bail, she said'.

I gave him a highly selective version of our exploits, omitting any reference to our steamy session in the hotel. That was our secret. Something to be savoured in moments of solitude. Not an item to be tossed casually into the conversation as if it were about a football match or a horse race. Some of the girls we tangled with were fair game, but this was something different.

Besides, I had seen the way Larry looked at her. Chris turned up later in the evening complaining of a wasted journey.

''She was on the rags. All I got was a couple of hand jobs. I could have done that myself. Besides, she got me there under false pretences. Said Bob Dylan was goin' to be playing…'

'And he wasn't?'

'Naw. It was that fucking Donovan…' He began to sing. 'They call me mellow yellow… what a wanker'.

He didn't seem surprised to hear about the money. 'Did she say what for?'

For her mother…or brother'. Larry gave him the details.

Chris laughed. 'Not her brother. She hasn't got one. Least, not called Ben'.

'How come you know so much about her all of a sudden?' I said, annoyed now that I had ever mentioned the money.

He shrugged. 'Little things I picked up. You can't spend time with people and not learn something. Human nature, isn't it?' He grinned. 'I suppose I'd better start looking for a new partner…'

As Jack finishes his story a blond-haired, statuesque woman appears in the doorway. Neither of them sees her for a moment, and then both of them do together.

JOHN: Tess…Tessa…

JACK: Ah, Theresa, there you are. Everybody, this is my wife, Theresa.

JOHN: (still bemused) Tess…Tessa…Theresa….Is, ah…your wife!

JACK: Theresa, this is John.

Silence for a moment.

JOHN: Delighted to meet you Theresa, haven't we met before someplace?

THERESA: No…No, I… I don't think so.

MICK: Ah now John, I'm sure if you met Theresa before, you would have a permanent memory of her, wouldn't you?

JOHN: Yes…yes Mick you're right, of course I would, and I might have even have penned a poem about her, Tess…Theresa, tell me why you didn't turn up…

Maggie interrupts John.

MAGGIE: Time now please, time now, everyone please, drink up or the guards will be in on top of us, okay. JOHN? Not now, leave it, leave it for another time

JOHN: Another time Maggie? Ah...shure you're right. The fella that made time made enough of it. But you don't expect us to leave our pints? Would you mind if we finish them off with a toast and a song?

MAGGIE: Yes John that would be good, a toast and a song.

John: Right lads a toast, to new friends, and old friends, and to friends who may have forgotten us, and to the next generation, and a Government for all the people, not just for some of the people

JACK: Right Mick give us a blast of The Parting Glass.

Of all the money that e'er I had
I've spent it in good company
And all the harm that e'er I've done
Alas it was to none but me
And all I've done for want of wit
To memory now I can't recall
So fill to me the parting glass
Good night and joy be with you all

Of all the comrades that e'er I had
They are sorry for my going away
And all the sweethearts that e'er I had
They would wish me one more day to stay
But since it falls unto my lot
That I should rise and you should not
I'll gently rise and I'll softly call
Good night and joy be with you all
Good night and joy be with you all

end

ABOUT THE AUTHORS

Tom O'Brien is a native of Kilmacthomas Co Waterford Ireland and is a full time writer and playwright. Performed plays include Money from America, Cricklewood Cowboys, On Raglan Road. Johnjo, Gorgeous Gaels, Brendan Behan's Women Down Bottle Alley etc Books include The Shiny Red Honda, Cassidy's Cross, Cricklewood Cowboys, The Waterford Collection. He has also recently published several collections of poetry. Tom lives in Hastings UK website: www.gorgeousgael.com All books are available on Amazon

Tom Power has been writing poems and short stories for many years, published in local magazines and newspapers, poems read on national and local radio. 'The Spoken Word' is a C/D of 22 poems. His one-act play 'Conversation in a Country Pub' was performed to officially open the Gealach Gorm Theatre in Kill, Co Waterford, his other one-act play 'The Mystery Letter' was also performed there. He has published two novels 'Dust Covered Memories' available on Amazon Kindle direct, and 'The Mysterious John Grey' available from www.feedaread.com   Tom lives in Kill Co Waterford Ireland

80808114R00024